T0010127

CATCHING THE LIGHT

CATCHING THE LIGHT

JOY HARJO

THE 2021 WINDHAM-CAMPBELL LECTURE

YALE UNIVERSITY PRESS
NEW HAVEN AND LONDON

The *Why I Write* series is published
with assistance from the Windham-
Campbell Literature Prizes, which
are administered by the Beinecke Rare
Book and Manuscript Library at
Yale University.

Published with assistance from the
Mary Cady Tew Memorial Fund.

Yale University Press books may be
purchased in quantity for educational,
business, or promotional use.
For information, please e-mail
sales.press@yale.edu (U.S. office) or
sales@yaleup.co.uk (U.K. office).

Printed in Great Britain.

Library of Congress Control
Number: 2022934816
ISBN 978-0-300-25703-8
(hardcover : alk. paper)

A catalogue record for this book is
available from the British Library.

This paper meets the requirements
of ANSI/NISO Z39.48-1992
(Permanence of Paper).

10 9 8 7 6 5 4 3 2 1

MIX
Paper from
responsible sources
FSC® C013056

CATCHING
THE LIGHT

I do not know when the first poem was, where it came from, or exactly how. I just know how much I needed it: the scrawl, the questioning, the words lining up in a musical sound sense to make something from the everything of nothing. I was in the dark and decided to investigate the dark to find the light.

I write to you now from Tulsa, Oklahoma, from the Mvskoke Creek Nation Reservation. We are at the border of three Native nations that also include the Osage and Cherokee. We honor and acknowledge those original keepers, past, present, and future, who care for these lands. We acknowledge the source of the gifts of our living, for without this Earth, or *Ekvnvcakv,* we would be without shelter, clothing, food, or inspiration. Consider that the Earth mind, architectures, and aesthetics shape the mother root of our imagination here.

*Vkvsamet hesaketmese pomvte. Mowe towekvs
pokvhoyen yiceyvte*

Mon vkerrickv heren. Pohkerricen vpeyeyvres

It was fifty years ago that I began this word venture, as an undergrad student at the University of New Mexico, a single mother with two children (and sometimes three), who went to school full-time, starting out as a pre-med major with a minor in dance, and changing the first year to studio art, my original career intent. I became involved with the Native student club, the Kiva Club, and met real Native poets and writers like Simon Ortiz and Leslie Marmon Silko.

I was introduced to the writing community in Albuquerque through Simon and Leslie, and through the stream of performances and activity at the Living Batch Bookstore across Central in front of the university, and through the English Department, which hosted a series of poets ranging from Galway Kinnell, whose poem "The Bear" gave me permission to write toward transformation, to Ai, whose mysterious yet eyes-wide-open poems made a road that led to bravery.

It was in the lands of the Southwest that poetry found its way to me, in words that were given context and lift from red mesas, piñon trees, and a light filtered by mountains, where so many left prayers through eons of history. The Southwest taught me an attention to light, to the arrangement of mountains and high plains. I could see the sky and even beyond the sky. And I was coming to learn that words were ladders, with each rung leading between the darkest of hours to sunlight, from confusion to accomplishment, or in the opposite direction.

I worked long hours with my research position at American Indian Studies, and my full-time slate of classes, and the day-to-day childcare. The night became my solitude. I have always needed solitude, yearned for it when it was scarce. I'd stay up nights painting and drawing, and then poetry elbowed its way in, when I thought I had no more room. My long nights then became a tug-of-war between poetry, artwork, and figuring out how my little family would make it on nearly nothing. My first poems were published a year later. In 2022 it will be fifty years since my first published poems.

This treatise will be something of a journey, about the why of writing poetry. There will be fifty vignettes, some poem-centered; others are points of illumination or questioning. In these fifty years, I have come to conclude that, ultimately, it is about catching light in the dark. Poetry (and other forms of writing) can be useful as a tool for finding the way into or through the dark. Or a device with which to admire the complexity of the stories in which we have become entangled. Sometimes

the only way out is by voice, following the music into
the impossible.

1

When my third granddaughter's body was forming, I watched and listened to what was going on in the atmosphere, to find a clue about this incoming family member, what she would need once she arrived here to take on her part of the story.

A powerful story was making the rounds in the Native community where I was living in New Mexico. There was a Navajo woman of a righteous nature who lived far out on the reservation in a *hogan*, the traditional home of the Navajo, or Diné people, there. She still prayed every morning with cornmeal, tended the altars of the living, took care of her sheep, and was loved and well respected by her relatives and neighbors. She was also blind. She was visited one day by the Holy Ones. As her hogan filled with the powerful presence of sacredness, the Holy Ones told her, as they towered over her, that they had come to give a warning to the people.

We are nearing times where we will experience Earth

changes, famine, and strife, because people are forgetting their original teachings.

The Holy Ones instructed her to tell everyone to keep hold of their traditional ways, which meant attending to prayer and minding their attention in all things, because it matters for the outcome of the people, for all life forms on this Earth. Without it, they will suffer.

The traditional ways and rituals of all of Earth's peoples are kept in containers of poetry, song, and story. It is how we know who we are, where we are coming from and who we are becoming.

I knew that my granddaughter was bringing in special gifts that would assist with these times we are moving into, times in which we are reckoning with our lack of respect and attention to what matters in this place.

I told this story at a performance in Flagstaff, Arizona, near one of the sacred mountains. Many of the Diné people there nodded their heads in remembering. For Holy Ones to touch down in that manner is powerful and dangerous; everyone must pay attention.

Afterward one of the women came up to me and remarked, "I saw the footprints of the Holy Ones in the sand in front of the hogan! They were very long and narrow."

The times the Holy Ones spoke of—we are now in those times. In this time at the crossroads of brokenness, we are watching and listening for what stories will nourish us.

At this cliff edge of becoming, there will be no turning back.

These are the times that invite tricksters who disturb the waters. It was in a time like this that Robert Johnson, blues guitarist, met the devil at the crossroads one humid night somewhere in the dark of history. It is in times like these that we face the most cunning of tricksters. We might even find a trickster in the seat of power. We have always had clowns and tricksters in every culture. They inhabit the power places because their role is to remind us that though we may hold and even wield power, power does not belong to us. It is meant to be shared.

2

This morning, an old friend from my days in the Kiva Club sent me an image. It is morning in Lukachukai, a mountainous region on the Navajo Reservation marked by piñon pines and mesa vistas. His sister is warming the truck before they take it down the mountain for their jobs. I smell strong coffee, hear the radio static in Navajo language from the truck's dash. A misty female rain has been brought as a gift from the sky to Earth. When he writes to me via FB Messenger, he writes in prayer language. By "prayer language," what I mean is that there is attention to the atmosphere of place and time, and how language is happening. Language is a living being. It is feeding this image, giving it a place to live in my imagination, even as the image calls forth language to speak on behalf of the beauty weaving the mountain and the sky, the beauty being breathed by my friend, his sister, and the livestock.

I came to writing poetry because I needed a language that was beyond ordinary. I was not a speaker.

I was the silent one who sat in the back, often caught up with invisible wars from fresh present to a historical past that revealed itself to me in shards and waves. I spoke everyday language, a colonized English. I consider English a language of trade. It enables us to understand each other across languages. The root languages of the Western Hemisphere are indigenous languages. These languages carry in them the plants of the area, star maps and meaning, directions concerning danger and safety, the how and meaning of becoming. English can be a language of alliance, of connection. During the ferocious efforts to destroy indigenous peoples, however, it attempted to overcome our languages. It acted as an enemy.

That we still have our Mvskoke language is a tribute to those who took care of culture. Our practice of our cultures was outlawed until 1978, when the Religious Freedom Act was passed on behalf of Native tribal nations.

3

1967 was quite a year. My origin story of writing poetry would begin here, after I arrived in Santa Fe at the Institute of American Indian Arts (IAIA), which was then a Bureau of Indian Affairs residential arts high school with a two-year postgraduate program. We were Native students from tribal nations throughout what is now called the United States, all of us there because of a demonstrated proficiency in the arts.

That fall when I began at IAIA, there were race riots across the country. The Vietnam War was blazing. Jimi Hendrix's first album, *Are You Experienced,* was released. Jim Morrison and the Doors followed with "Light My Fire," and Thurgood Marshall was sworn in as the first Black justice of the U.S. Supreme Court. The free-love explosion was traveling from Haight-Ashbury in San Francisco all over the country, including Santa Fe's Canyon Road. Native rights movements were stirring in the wake of the Civil Rights Movement, and Alcatraz would soon be occupied. I arrived at the main dorm on the Cerrillos Road campus of IAIA with my metal army footlocker, carrying everything I owned from Tulsa. When I walked up that wide, tall porch and signed in, I did not look back.

In the months before, I had seriously considered running away to San Francisco. I needed out of the abusive situation at home, but I was underage and had no credibility as a young Native woman. As I considered that runaway path, I had a sense that it would lead to an early death on the street. I was not savvy. When despair overtook me, I found refuge in drawing and in music. I searched for a path to the doorways offered by artistic practice. Art was natural in me, a constant. I told my mother I wanted to go to Indian school, and at the Indian agency in Muskogee I was slated to attend Chilocco Indian School until my mother mentioned that I was an artist. The agent handed her a brochure of the new arts program at IAIA. I clutched that brochure like a life preserver, made my application with drawings, and was accepted. With that enrollment, I felt a kind of grace appear, an interception, an affirmation of a path toward a future.

I know of the power of arts personally, and as a person of my generation. As a child growing up in Oklahoma, I was aware of our Native peoples as artists. In my home I was inspired by the oil paintings of my grandmother, Naomi Harjo, a full-blood and a deeply cultural Mvskoke Creek. She also played saxophone in Indian Territory before Oklahoma was a state. One of my most prized possessions is her painting of Osceola, the Seminole warrior who was our uncle by marriage. Because my grandmother passed of tuberculosis long before I was born, her sister, my aunt Lois Harjo, mentored me. She was also a painter in oils. She worked at the Creek Council House and taught art to community members.

There was a place in our communities for artists. Being an artist was something a young Native child could aspire to, as most of us had relatives who worked publicly and respectfully as artists. I grew up knowing of Jerome Tiger, Benjamin West, Solomon McCombs, and Maria Tallchief. Arts were what our people excelled in—it was expected of us. We were present in arts, though our history was not taught and we faced daily discrimination.

In the 1960s the Cherokee artist Lloyd Kiva New had a vision of fostering the talent of young Native artists, and developing the field of indigenous arts. In 1963 Kiva and his team were instrumental in opening IAIA, and so began a watershed age of accomplishment and transformation, when Native arts and artists would achieve national and world context and recognition.

What I found there was a refuge, and more than that, a family made up of other Native students from all over the country, and our arts teachers, all of us on the artist path together. In that incarnation of IAIA, we still had, lined up against the wall in one of my classrooms, stoves that had been used just a few years earlier to teach female students how to clean and cook for town residents. And out back, a dairy barn structure for teaching male students how to farm. When it was time for inoculations, half the student body would run to escape behind those buildings.

The staff could be our biggest allies. I got up at 5:00 every morning to work the kitchen detail because of the Pueblo woman who ran the kitchen. We worked hard, but laboring under her diligent care and presence gave me a sense of family. The school's guidance staff pulled together when any of us went down. They were both our counselors and the police. We often crashed hard.

Every weekend was a challenge for all of us to make it through the rough terrain of historical trauma. Students went missing, overdosed, or broke down. We'd all help each other not get caught. One Saturday night I almost didn't make it. I clung to the wall between the bathrooms and my dorm room, as I began sliding to the floor in an overdose. I kept telling myself that if I was found there, they would send me home. I mustered the strength to crawl to my room, climb into my bed, and pass out from the drugs I had mixed with alcohol.

If I were to be sent home, I knew I would die. I would rather live and die here, in peace.

The teachers of academics were either the best and most dedicated because they loved Natives and had pride in their work. Or they were there because they had exhausted other avenues and couldn't be hired anywhere else. These were the most eccentric. One world history teacher spent much of the semester addressing nudity in ancient Egypt.

Our arts teachers were the finest available, both Native and non-Native. We learned under the Apache sculptor Allan Houser; painting and drawing under Fritz Scholder, Mission Indian; studied traditional pottery with Otellie Loloma, Hopi, and graphic arts with Seymour Tubis; learned traditional techniques with Josephine Myers-Wapp, Comanche; theater with Rolland Meinholtz; and many more.

Louis Ballard was Quapaw/Cherokee from Oklahoma, and a renowned composer of classical music at IAIA. He composed for Maria Tallchief, among others, and was one of the first to weave traditional tribal music with European classical styles. He was assigned as my adviser. When I started writing and performing music, he became one of my biggest champions. I think of him now as I write the script and the music for a musical play that will tell the tale of a young Mvskoke

Creek musician named Justice Fields and his band, as he discovers how his people are part of the origin story of American music, comes to terms with the history of theft by oil companies in his family, and battles a heroin addiction.

Though we were young, we had a sense of destiny among ourselves. Our ancestors had imagined us with pride, and we felt an urgency to cultivate and celebrate those cultural gifts. Each of us had found challenge, inspiration, and redemption in practicing our arts as individuals, as members of clans, tribal bands, and Nations. Yet even as our eyes shone with possibility, we arrived there dragging loss, trauma, and grief from all corners of a history that had been enacted against us in the name of Manifest Destiny. The phrase "historical trauma" hadn't emerged in the vernacular then, but we were direct evidence of it. Many of us were becoming aware that we had come into a time ripe for a collective, national change of identity and personhood.

We were that generation in the late 1960s that began to change everything as we questioned who we were as young Native artists, as tribal members with roots in classical tribal thought and culture—who were being inspired, should I say "turned on," by what was happening in the large field of American culture(s). We were the generation that changed the face of American

Indian art as we challenged stereotypes and tropes that prophesized our extinction. We found groundbreaking ways to make fresh paths over our ancient trails of concept, design, and architecture.

What I learned as a student at IAIA in the late 1960s became central to my consequent journey as a Mvskoke poet, writer, playwright, musician, and teacher. We were inspired and directed to make our original art, born of major traditions in arts and cultures, even as we were venturing out for fresh ideas, images. We were wounded, but it was in the wounding that we would find our strength. As we practiced our arts, we realized that we had a hand in revising the story of who we are as indigenous nations, who we were, and who we were becoming. We would come to learn that our indigenous arts and lifeways are crucial to a healthy and dynamic American story. There is no America without us. And our arts, the arts of all our citizens, show the way to a meaningful future.

4

At the heart of every creation is a need to connect, even if it is to connect to no one in silent defiance or a curious desperation. The inner world is even more immense than the measured world we have created out of wants, hunger, and sometimes, need. Every word marks an act of creation, an intent, and often not a studied intent. We make ceremony with words even as our words can lead us to the hells of destruction. This is one of the most potent teachings of the earliest attempts at writing poetry. I have come to see the process as a kind of call-and-response. Silence calls out, as do the kinds of voices that can be heard only when silence is present.

The poet listens with pen, pencil in hand, or hands poised above the typewriter or keyboard, adrift in the orality of making words and finding out where they are going. I feel compelled to use the symbology of words, phrases, sound, music, and metaphorical import. It's a back and forth. The road isn't always clear. There can be jams, wrecks of questions, belief on its knees, mountains of sand, or fires — and you learn with practice that these are part of it. We can go under, over, through, or around. Or be lost. The Laguna Pueblo novelist and poet Leslie Silko, in her stories and poems, often references the storyteller who, one day, was so immersed in the story that she disappeared in the story, never to be found. She essentially becomes the story.

5

When I was a student at IAIA, I never took any of the creative writing classes. I was a studio art student who found her way to the drama and dance classes and became a member of one of the earliest American Indian drama troupes.

These performances began with attention to words, and how they evoked movement, gesture, and meaning. To perform, I learned that the storehouses of silence that I carried within my slight, youthful body could be useful when it came to expressing a character or characters in the playhouse of good and evil.

An actor is a walking metaphorical being. They are who they are as an accumulation of knowledge and presence merging at a crossroads of time and age, and they are yet another possibility of being who finds expression through them, a being brought into the present by words. Artists are aware of the metaphorical aspect of their creations, they sense that their work is prayer — not a prayer to the white, patriarchal, angry god of judgment, but an immersion in a flood of creative brilliance, larger than the human imagination.

We are all as actors, wearing the masks of family, generation, or occupation. We step into the story when we take our first breath. We will lay down the masks when we return to the spiritual jumping-off place.

6

Though the generations lost in virtual worlds and texting may not agree, to connect in person is more potent and powerful. There is less ability to lie and be deceptive. Words are accompanied by clothes of gestures, expressions, tonality. We are in a living communicative atmosphere, even if communication by words fails or leads to misunderstanding; the field of our communal communication is dynamic. Consider what happens when a live poetry reading or music performance morphs to the audio of the radio, then next, the audio is married to the visual as in music videos, then becomes virtually immersive with earbuds or headphones when the listener is alone on an island of perception. Consider what happens when reading silently and alone. There's a difference in experience that takes you further away from the presence of living word.

Consider the distillation of experience in texting. Words are abbreviated. Symbols and acronyms are the gestures. There is no long slope that allows communion.

We lose out on a wider band of perception along the way. Yet if you turn this construction upside down, you might argue otherwise. The symbolic undergirding of texting is a coding with expansive leeway. With our audio devices and books, we can carry worlds with us, and we are connected. Communal experience makes community, even if it is virtual and experienced in solitude. Still, breathing together, speaking, and listening make a more solid ritual, a grounding. I do not want to live my life in virtual images or by artificial sound. I prefer the messiness of physical living. Babies crying in the audience, someone coughing and getting up to leave, children whispering as they play with crayons and toys brought to distract them.

7

Poetry first appeared in my life as an oral event. My mother spoke and sang poetry in the everyday of our living. Through this speak-singing, I began to consider the expression of poetry as an entity, a being.

My mother sang her poetry, and as she sang, the images and words through her voice made a living story presence.

Songwriting was natural for my mother and was how she revealed her deepest, unspeakable self. I heard how deeply she loved my father and how she suffered for that love. She wrote on an Underwood typewriter, the most compelling object I had ever seen. It was a magic word machine! With it she created entities called songs that traveled throughout the house to embrace, even protect, us when the schism between her imagined love and the reality of my father's capriciousness grew uncrossable. She would go into a local studio and make demos to send to Hollywood for publishing.

In those earliest years, before I was seven, we knew

and sang all the top hits on the radio. Lyrics surfed chordal structures with melody. My mother recited the poetry she had learned in the one-room schoolhouse she had attended while growing up in a sharecropper family at the border of Oklahoma and Arkansas. Her favorite poet was William Blake. We put the words to foot action and jitterbugged to Buddy Holly or later did the Twist with Fats Domino. We ached with Patsy Cline and her song "Crazy" and fell in love with the croon of Nat King Cole. It was all connected, this poetics of listening, word making, and dancing. There was power to transform, to lighten the heaviness of the burden of being human. That's how I came to understand the power of poetry and music. It was a tool, but more than a tool. Words and music evoked a state of mind that lifted us up when racial and historical despair threatened.

8

My mother's predominant song genre was ballads. They were written as her beloved wandered from us into the arms of women, sometimes her friends, in the same clubs in which they had met, partied, and danced together. I accidentally wrote "into the arms of ghosts" instead of "arms of women" in the above sentence, because what inspired my father's need to wander was his being torn from his mother when she was put away first for tuberculosis, then by death. This was before he had words or an understanding large enough to encompass the hurt. His wordlessness made a kind of mother-ghost that haunted him all of his days.

My father grew up in a twenty-one-room house bought with Indian oil money, then was sent to a military school in Ponca City by his father and stepmother, not long after his stepmother brought her own family of boys into the house when his mother died. I never heard my father quote poetry or sing. His silence was the speaker. Words were utilitarian and for the most part did not belong to him, a then young Native father who was lost in a society that was constructed over his culture. He was marooned between English and Mvskoke. He passed on to me the urgency to find a way out and through. It was unspoken. He was a dancer. I feel the same thrill move through my feet that moved through his when music took hold, in the dark, after the lights were turned down. My way became poetry and eventually, music. In poetry there is that same thrill when the music takes hold.

9

My first published poem as an undergraduate student at the University of New Mexico was formed from anguish. It was not yet a poem, even as it appeared to be a poem. Like starts for tomato plants or zucchini, I had been writing poem-starts on bar napkins to open conversation, like looking around the room and wondering where everyone came from and how they wound up here on this corner of desperation. Natives are always asking: "Where you from?" I'd write lyrical notes to decipher the messages that emerged through the mess of colonized wilderness, sometimes even a startled S.O.S. signal.

I was a university student, arriving on campus after a year of major antiwar demonstrations that had galvanized the student community. The National Guard had been called out. Native rights movements were beginning to emerge, especially in the Plains and upper Midwest. At the University of New Mexico we were mostly southwestern Native peoples, from the pueblos perched along the edges of the Rio Grande, or the Athabascan Navajo and Apache peoples to the south and west. There were a few of us Oklahoma Indians, including a handful of other Mvskoke, and others from tribal nations all over the country.

Many of us were within a generation of coming up in traditions of orality, of knowledge systems that managed to survive nearly intact if not in shards. What held it all together appeared to be grease and humor, and always a deep sense of awe and respect for life, for this thing called living.

There was the Indian bar across town where I was often being eyed for a fight by other women. Another bar for dancing was farther up on Central, which was across the street from the gay bar with the best music and a dance floor of color-lit plexiglass. The preferred hangout was Okies. It was close to the university, and it was the Indian, biker, and poet bar, a direct line to higher education. We all met there to vision together or apart on beer, wine, and whatever else we found and brought through the doors, swinging through the nights at the corner of Yale and Central. Mainly it was just to get together, tell stories, laugh, and hang out. In the beginning, I wasn't old enough to enter those doors legally. And even then, some places still wouldn't serve American Indians alcohol. That's a different story.

Most of our Native student community never

set foot in any of these places. I grew up in a family in which bars were the community social gathering places, though it never worked out well in the end. I've come to believe that they are so attractive because they hold stories, jukeboxes, or bands that share songs. We need stories, music, and companionship to feed our spirits. Add the loosening up elements of alcohol and pool games and a bar can be a refuge. Yet it can also be a tricky island of forgetfulness. It's dangerous. You can easily go too far or get trapped into returning night after night, to repeat a high that will never be the same again. After a few hours in this atmosphere, I would feel I belonged. I could be myself on the dance floor. This kind of high has a wide-open trap door if there is no one or nothing there to catch you.

My first poem came from navigating the party after the party, the one for the hardcore who had no place else to go but despair. Those parties could happen in someone's home or on the street. I won't name the poem. It was an attempt to salvage the embers of living. The poem was not strong enough to hold it.

Like everyone else there, I was looking for a vision, for freedom from the ugliness of shame and loathing. I was looking for a language to speak my way out of there, hence the scribbling on bar napkins, my face covered by my long hair. I made a cave of silence in the mess and found poetry there.

10

I began my studio art studies at the University of New Mexico during a time of burgeoning national Native consciousness. In the long hours as I painted through the night, I would replay the stories and testimonies I heard in our Kiva Club meetings on campus, the stories we heard when we were out in the surrounding communities working together for social justice issues. We heard reports of moral violations that were destroying our tribal lands, our relatives, our brothers and sisters, our lifeways. We frequently sat in meetings with the power brokers whose decisions would decide the fate of peoples, waters, and lands. It became obvious that there were separate realities of oppositional values and worldviews. As Native peoples we were up against those who believed that power and value lay in the acquisition of lands, fuels, and natural resources. They believed Earth to be a dead thing, meant only to be mined of anything that would bring money into the hands of the power players. Earth is a living being. We cannot own the

Earth; rather we are an essential part of the Earth. Our relationship with the Earth will decide the fate of our families, our future generations. To dig, destroy, take more than you need, and to do so with the intent to benefit a few is considered disrespectful to all, and more than that, extremely dangerous.

I was impressed by the testimonies of the elder keepers of traditions whose presences and testimonies were eloquent, never over-reaching or of greedy intent. They spoke as protectors. They spoke humbly. The questions arise in me now, as they did then — why do we continue to have to battle for protection of our home, this Earth garden? Why do the destroyers appear to have the odds no matter which way we turn for justice? It was in that listening where the impulse was born in me to turn to the making of poetry, to make word trails that could lead to justice. The awareness of language as a tool for justice, survival, beauty, and persistence began to sing in me. The combination of social justice, on-the-ground focus, and the possibility of speaking in our own literary constructions and voices as Native peoples struck an unknown in me, and I followed it.

One of my poems from that time emerged after one of the leaders of our American Indian student club passed in a freak accident, leaving behind a young daughter. I had admired her attention to what mattered, her grace, her beauty even as she stood quiet and studied against the evil that wished to take every resource and turn it into money. She had organized, passed out fly-ers, had been present at every protest. I wish that I could say that the poem I wrote in her honor had the power to overturn the destroyers. I like to believe that it helped her daughter and the rest of us to continue walking forward, and to continue weaving a story that would remind us of the beauty, no matter how we and this Earth are tested.

11

Years ago, when I was starting out on the poetry road, and trying to find a way to make a living, I took on many small residencies, commissions, and opportunities. When I was asked if I could write a screenplay for a screenwriting job, I said yes, made a quick study of how to write screenplays, and wrote a script for a one-hour story that became a favorite in the White Mountain Apache community for which it was commissioned. While I was still an undergrad I began working in poetry-in-the-school programs in New Mexico and then continued teaching poetry in elementary, middle, and high schools in Oklahoma and Arizona. In the early 1980s I was asked to be part of a poetry-in-prisons project in Alaska. I was given an itinerary that included four prisons and jails in Anchorage and the nearby area. I had to rent a car and because I had no credit card, I had to use cash for a deposit at the local Rent-a-Wreck. They gave me a used police car, which could have seriously damaged my credibility as I drove up and parked at each facility.

My first assignment was the Fourth Avenue jail. The jailer walked me to a secure room. Inside was a long table around which were seated several inmates, mostly Native and Black men. He said, "I will be back in two hours," and locked the door behind him as he left me there. I had books of poetry. The inmates and I shared poetry. Most of them knew poetry by heart. They shared it, then wrote new poetry, read it. We laughed and cried together. The only interruption was when an inmate was called out to mop up the blood of another inmate in his cell. This experience was similar to my other site visits. I came to understand that most of the prisoners would not have been there if they had the funds to afford skilled representation or were not dark-skinned or otherwise Native. I met one of my Indian school student's brothers in the area prison. He was there for something not prison-worthy — a joint of marijuana, or being in the wrong place at the wrong time. I came to realize that my presence there with poetry was to remind them of the value of the poetry within each of them, planted there before the colonizers established jails and prisons. No matter where they were or what happened, poetry could be a refuge, as well as a place to hide the songs they couldn't sing because doing so would make them even more suspect, add years to their time. Poetry then, was anchorage.

12

The United Nations' Convention on the Prevention and Punishment of the Crime of Genocide, adopted in 1948, defines genocide as "acts committed with intent to destroy, in whole or in part, a national, ethnical, racial or religious group." It is a crime under international law. The phrase "cultural genocide" is not particularly used, but in the definition, genocide may include anything causing serious mental harm to a group, according to Chief Justice Beverley McLachlin in a 2015 speech she gave in Vancouver. She was referring to Canada's treatment of its Aboriginal people and explained that "cultural genocide" began in the colonial period.

Cultural genocide occurs directly, when a people's language, cultural ways of moving about and knowing the world, are systematically destroyed, when the roots — the children — are taken away to be raised in a system that lacks nourishment.

Within a few generations of the first immigrant settlements in this country, the population of Native peoples has gone from nearly 100 percent of the population of this country to less than half of 1 percent. We are not present as human beings. We exist predominately in the form of stereotypes, as sports mascots. "Redskins" is a deeply rooted image that is proving nearly impossible to dislodge. The term refers to the bodies of Natives brought in for bounty by those who wanted us removed. This travesty of representation would not be allowed for any other cultural group in this country, yet for Natives, it remains — even though there would be no America without us, without our contributions to the American form of democracy, to American arts, cultures, and humanities. We are not apparent in the cultural streams that establish and define American thought, art, and culture. We are not present at the table, though we appear perpetually at the table every Thanksgiving in stories told to our children in educational institutions across the country. But Natives were not there at that table. There was no table. Their heads were on stakes giving warning around the newly constructed towns by the settlers, built on Native lands.

These false narratives of Native peoples continue a story of cultural genocide.

We are in a crisis. These same false narratives have fostered a destruction of the natural environment in which we live, and grow children, grandchildren — in which we make a world in which to continue. What joins the original cultures of these lands is a shared belief system in which we are not separate from the land or from the consequences of the stewardship of these lands. These lands aren't my lands. These lands aren't your lands. We are the land. Together we move and move about with the knowledge that we are not at the top of a hierarchy; rather, we are part of an immense field of knowledge and beingness, and human contribution, though crucial, is not the most important. All have a place. What use do humans have in this bio system? Are we necessary to Earth's ecology?

Writing itself is an act of affirmation, even of sovereignty. We confirm that we are human beings, that we are alive and making and breathing culture. I often think of that woman in my poem who was hanging from the thirteenth-floor window in Chicago, and of her family. I wonder what poems she is making, what art, because she found a way to climb back up again.

13

As scribes of our generation, we are called to remember what matters. We always begin the story with the land: how it is regarded, our relationship to it, and how we move about on it, how we honor the keepers of the land, and how we give back. Our materials, from baskets, painting and sculpture implements, instruments, inspirations, designs, architectural concepts, song concepts and stories, are directly tied to some aspect of land, landscape, and place. Many of our origin stories involve emergence from the land, or they detail how we arrive here in this place. Our relationship to the land defines how we understand our place in the world. Our cultural stories live within our DNA and unwind throughout our lifetimes, as singular entities and as Native nations and countries.

One Mvskoke origin story (the Mvskoke Nation is a confederacy of many smaller tribal towns and cultures, bound together by geography, history, and belief) says that we emerged from darkness into this place where we were given everything we needed. We are cautioned to take care of what was given to us. We share Turtle Island with all plants, animals, and natural forces. When we veer from tending that connection, then we dim the light. When we build walls at borders, we destroy the light within all of us. When our need for oil destroys the homes of caribou and polar bears, then we are destroyed.

What kind of Inupiat culture would there be without ice, whales, and cultural paths of movement and renewal?

During a convening of Native Arts and Cultures Foundation mentors, an Anishinaabe mentor, Wayne Minogiizhig Valliere, said: "We're not losing the birch trees, the birch trees are losing us."

To regard the Earth, or *Ekvnvcakv,* as a person, as a mother, is not a romantic notion. Understanding this will be essential to our survival. To understand this relationship means that we have respect for life, for the mother principle, for women who stand alongside men, not beneath them. In this collective Earth crisis, we are experiencing the outcome of disconnection, of breaking the universal laws that appear in original teachings of most cultures in the world: Do not take more than you can use. Respect life. Respect the giving of life. And give back.

Like many other Natives, I have resisted efforts to make the idea of our personhood synonymous with the land, because in past narratives it has been used to dehumanize us. In the Papal Bull of 1450, Pope Nicholas V issued to King Afonso V of Portugal the Romanus Pontifex, declaring war against all non-Christians throughout the world, and specifically sanctioning and promoting the conquest, colonization, and exploration of non-Christian nations and their territories. Pope Nicholas V directed King Afonso to "capture, vanquish, and subdue the Saracens, pagans, and other enemies of Christ," to "put them into perpetual slavery," and "to take all their possessions and property."

Cultural genocide means the destruction of the cultural legacy of what is American. There is no America without all our tribal nations, without the acknowledgment of our arts, cultures, and humanities, without the rich and varied contributions of the people and communities of these nations.

Despite the history, the cultural repression and attempts to make us disappear, the damage and even carnage, we have persisted. We are resilient. Within our arts, cultures, and expressions of humanity, we have tended and envisioned ourselves as full members of resilient and living cultures. We are in the present. Our cultural and artistic creations have freshly rooted images, sounds, and stories that can restore the American story, that can assist in the care and respect of the environment and in the betterment of quality of life for human beings and the Earth herself, *Ekvnvcakv*.

The Old Ones urge and remind us, remember. Remember to remember.

14

The first time I visited New Orleans I was in my late twenties or early thirties, there as a grants panelist for a literary organization called Coordinating Council of Literary Magazines. I was there for public service, but more profoundly, the journey was about coming home. New Orleans was the closest I had come to what had been traditional Muscogean tribal nation territory, included in the states of Louisiana, Mississippi, Tennessee, Alabama, Georgia, and Florida, from which our peoples had been forcibly removed by President Andrew Jackson. It was my first time in that humid air. I breathed deeply as I stood along that fat snake of a hungry river, and knew this place now called "New Orleans" was a kind of energetic transformer station within me. I drank it all in — that place, the history, the stories remembered and forgotten then dredged up again by music, by poetry.

Behind and within us — each of us, individuals and cultural entities — stands a long line of dreamers, artists, and thinkers. One line of my family, whose story I am, crossed the big river far north of New Orleans, near Memphis. Others crossed closer to the Crescent City. In that city, specifically in Congo Square, lives the origin story of blues, jazz, and rock. This music came about because of the cultural exchange that happened between the indigenous peoples who lived and met there. It was always a crossroads of peoples and cultures, long before Jean-Baptiste Le Moyne de Bienville left France to establish a new community in a new world.

The Mvskoke people were and are part of this cultural awakening. The circle of influence that led to the creation of this new music has been cited by musicologists and other historians as primarily the undertaking of West African and European peoples and cultures. Indigenous peoples are always left out of the story, though there is no story without place — and there would be no blues, jazz, or rock if there had not been a Muscogean tribal nation village, a Houma village, the congregation place for West Africans who found family there because of cultural similarities. Because of the location of that Houma village by the big river, many tribal visitors came through there when traveling north and south, or east and west, for trade and for all the usual reasons that human beings travel and have traveled throughout time. There would be no new American music without Native contributions.

It was a timeless kind of time, when the fire at that Houma village was initiated, when songs were laid down there, and when fresh insight and forms emerged from negotiations between styles and rhythms. It was not for money or fame that the music was created. Corn grows better with intention and song. As do all plants. As do our children. As may any entity whose resonance can respond to the calling of the forces of music.

We know much of the powerful musical invention and breakthrough that happened in this river city. It continues morphing into new forms and fresh expression. Poetry is never far from music, nor is dance.

This is essential to my genealogy as a poet and musician. It is my inheritance.

I consider that many of my poetry and music ancestors came through this city through the generations. Most kept on going to Oklahoma, and some went as far as California. Louis Armstrong is a jazz ancestor, a kind of great-grandfather, or even an Adam of jazz, with Billie Holiday nearby as a stunning and gifted Eve. What fed all of them was the music of the Mississippi River, an entity that continues to carry life and stories from the north to the south, emptying into the Gulf of Mexico with arms to encircle the Caribbean. That river is a poem fed by the Arkansas that flows by my home south of Tulsa.

Rivers carry the emotional waves of culture. The

Trail of Tears crossed the Mississippi River and then took the Arkansas River west. This is also the trail made by the story of American music. How the waters were stirred up by the music, dance, and poetry circle that emerged at Congo Square, from peoples of many African cultures, many indigenous cultures, and a few Europeans! They were all musicians, poets, and culture bearers — people whose ears are always traveling out to hear what they haven't heard before, to take in what is being said, passed on, given by inspiration, from those realms without words.

I look for lost pieces of the story, for what has been untold because there were not the words or the ability to speak. Some stories cannot exist within incompatible resonances cut by time or history. No one sees the indigenous of these lands anywhere, but we are here, have been and always will be. Listen to the music.

15

The most ubiquitous of poems are love poems. They are written to find another word for love, for the divine, the impossible, the ecstatically present. They are written to call one to oneself, a kind of shamanistic purpose. Or, when love has escaped or disappeared, to speak of love lost, broken, or of the bereft floating in the sea of lostness.

Just as in love poems, all poems, stories, songs are about connection. Are you here, where are you, who am I without you, are you still there?

I consider every poem a kind of love poem. I am called to write as if each stroke to make a letter is a beat. Everything begins and ends with rhythm. Bay-be, bay-be, bay-be. When you coming home? You've been gone so long. I keep the porch light on for you. And when I'm gone sing that song for me, the one that praises your old run-down car that took us everywhere when we were young and thought we knew everything, and we didn't know nothing.

The breathing as I write is a beat. My heart is the interchange of rivers, so many rivers run through this body. The beat is an iambic line that turns into circles of resonant waves, after the word is thrown like a stone into the river of life.

16

Because of the violent interference of aggressive settlers who took over our lands in a relatively short time, we appeared to be culturally gutted. When sacred places cannot be maintained, we wander. The sacredness is put away until the songs can be heard again, in the right order, and when the precise unfolding of time is most nourishing. We continue to carry these places and possibilities in our songs, our poetry, and our instructions. Our imaginations are ripe with teachings, with love and respect for those ancestors who knew and still know the particulars of how to be human. Yet it was those who stayed close to the fire, those who lived within our languages, who appeared to fail in the American system. It is there we find ourselves, though sometimes uneasily with the English language. When we speak that tongue, we might sound like winds stirred by chaos and war.

Repetition is a mnemonic device that is essential to circling around the fire and makes for emphatic remembering. I do not know why the phrase "she had some horses" came and took me with it, when I was far away from horses, though always close to the love of horses. I was raised in a small postwar neighborhood, without corrals or ranches, without enough land for horses, and with city ordinances forbidding them. Yet they were there with me, presences who were given form and agency generations back as they were tamed and used for transportation.

Or did they appear to humans and tolerate and tame us?

The oldest stories I have are of my great-grandfather, six times, who was known for his horsemanship. There may have been others before him, others whose names have not been remembered. I saw him once on his favorite horse. I heard him first as he emerged from family memory, coming up behind me as I merged onto that southern interstate after leaving the battlefield grounds where he had suffered seven gunshot wounds, and the loss of one of his wives and their children. (Many had several wives then, partly to care for those who would have been without support, because of pestilence, massacres, and wars.) I felt the rhythm, the pounding of the Earth, a kind of song. Then I saw them approach, this powerful horse and rider, and watched as they ran alongside the car. My grandfather and his horse appeared to be one, a kind of apparition given breath by memory. He was not a large man, though his presence belied his actual physical size. His mind was constructed differently than my English-shaped mind. Yet we were and are connected by blood, and blood does not need words in which to speak. He disappeared into the mists of story as I continued moving into a continuation of it. He had some horses. She who followed him, therefore, had some horses.

17

In the early years of writing poetry, I faced the same kind of roadblocks as any other poet attempting to make poetry, lacking the experience with technique and craft yet holding an immense belief in the power of words. I read the hottest prevailing writers and poets; I reached back to their predecessors and read, listened, and pondered their work, then wrote forward to the impossible. The process is still pretty much the same, only deeper, and more mysterious. There are levels of mystery that emerge with practice and age. One of the rules of writing that stands throughout time: do not be complacent. Take risks. And most important, listen. Our ears are bent differently based on the culture, environment, and shape of the forming story as we exist in time and place. We flow from the many lines of ancestry we inherit, from family, practice, and place.

18

One of my first real poems appeared to my hands from my imagination to combat fear. It's not as if the poem suddenly appeared to me, as if in an aural vision, and I transcribed it. That's not exactly how poetry happens. The materials of a poem or a song come from many places, times, and even memories that might not be your own personal memories. The process of creation begins years before you approach the page or screen. It is a gathering together of perception and sound as you accumulate experience and knowledge on this road of becoming. A gesture will be evocative and implant itself, such as the eyes of a warrior as s/he turns from the last gaze at her/his beloved. Or a black butterfly who came with a message from someone just departed from Earth. Much is gained through nuance, through what is not said, in what is ineffable.

The tools for writing can be sharpened with listening, reading, and practice. The practice is ongoing.

I have always been attracted to poem-songs that

have a specific stated purpose, that are made to go out and accomplish a literal task. I think of Louis Oliver, Mvskoke poet who wrote a song in the shape of a snake who was more than a snake. Or translations of older songs from our traditions that can stop a storm, which I will not print here because they would be out of context in time, language, and place and could be dangerous in a distorted form. Love songs serve similarly, to praise a beloved, or to turn them in your direction. Just as breakup songs serve to sever, even act for revenge.

That fear poem came during those early days of writing, when I questioned why poetry found a most unlikely companion in me. I didn't fit anywhere. I was struggling as a full-time student. I had a job researching Native art and was raising two children alone. That was struggle enough; however, there was another plane of consciousness on which I was fighting every night that I lay down to rest. As I slid into the borderlands between waking and sleeping, negative beings attempted to pull me into their darkness. I learned to escape them by using words to make a ladder to bring me back. The words needed force from the gut to give enough power to emerge from their reach, to a place where these beings could no longer exist as a threat. I was told by my poetry self to lift myself up with words, with songs. They would change my being and I could no longer be destroyed by that which wanted to enslave or destroy me.

With each new poem, story, or song, I need to be challenged, opened to the impossible, then restored. This happens with a call-and-response between my spirit and the light of knowing. I ask questions, listen, then find the musical waves upon which to write. I never know where I am going or how I will get there, and that's the thrill of it.

19

If you look to the traditional power of using words, stories are for teaching, even entrancement, to carry forth memory as truth or fiction. Songs and oratory are used particularly for praise, grief, for planting, growing, to call love or someone to you. Songs can turn a storm, have the power to travel and to assist you while travelling, and are especially potent in your own indigenous language. Words can be manipulated into spells that can make someone pay attention to you, without their will. There are rules against using words to ensnare, or otherwise harm. All depend on oral delight to open a pathway. Every song or poem has purpose, or it would not be living.

20

You can teach the mechanics, the craft, the genres of poetry by referencing the ancestor texts of poetry or by studying the field according to theory, but you cannot make a poet. Poetry is not a career—it is a state of being. You become poetry or are in a state of becoming with poetry. My chronological map of becoming would not be linear, rather it has been crisscrossed with arcs of events, poems, poets, arts, music, all bound and directed by history and memory.

There is also an accompanying linear tale. I attended graduate school at the Iowa Writers' Workshop during two of the worst winters of the century. I often felt far away from poetry there because I was miles away from anything or anyone familiar.

Along the Iowa River, the world slowly froze in winter, and my relationship with the sun drastically changed. I learned that cultures fit to the landscape. I was farther north than I had ever been. The lack of sunlight was nearly devastating to this sun lover. I felt abandoned by the giver of life. Everything moved slower: the sky, exhaust from vehicles, my ability to write or dream. I was not graceful here.

I let the dark take me down.

I looked first for a Native community and found it in Meskwaki citizen Iva Roy, who was living in Iowa City, a few hours down the road from her home community, the Meskwaki Settlement. Their tribal nation's story is unique. After being chased by U.S. government forces, their lands stolen by the settlers in illegal deals brokered by the United States, the tribal members pooled their funds and bought lands in their homelands, outside the small town of Tama, Iowa. This Meskwaki history is part of the foundational root forming the bedrock of American poetry written in these lands. As a student, far from home, I found refuge there with Iva and her people.

My children were the same ages as hers and they ran the cornfields together. I found a home of laughter, good food, and familiarity.

In those bleak hours as I studied and wrote, I did not write in the way I had established for myself as a young poet. My poetry did not fit with what the Iowa Workshop praised as preferable in style and manner. The move was not only geographically uprooting, but it was also stylistically and philosophically challenging. If I had written from exactly where I was in the chaos of lostness, my new poems might have oddly found a fresh coherence. Instead, my poetry wore the clothes of strangers, and stuttered a new language, to try and fit in. It didn't work. It never will, not now or ever.

For a year I struggled with finding and making a home for my voice in that concrete-block student apartment of the long winters. I studied the poetry of Ray Young Bear, a Meskwaki poet from the settlement whose poems were cultural presences who found themselves uneasily but powerfully in English. When my voice crawled out into sunlight after that first hard winter, and stood up, I realized that the challenge would be to continue to find strength in difference. Unlike nearly everyone else in the workshop, I did not look to England or Europe as the baseline for knowledge and creation. We are the Americas. Yet I was writing in English and poetry was my way to speak Mvskoke presence, in poetry, a kind of word-bending round the corners of square houses and thoughts. Perhaps any indigenous person writing in a trade language must find alternate places of becoming, of insight, and inspiration.

I left Iowa, returned to New Mexico, and soon taught at the Institute of American Indian Arts, still a Bureau of Indian Affairs school, but the high school was being phased out. I taught the last year of high-school students, a small class of especially gifted students, artistically and spiritually. I was excited to be back in the sun rituals of the southern lands, with indigenous communities.

While I waited for my bags, the first time I returned to Iowa, several years later, I received a message that Iva Roy had died suddenly in Denver, where she had moved shortly after I had graduated, and her body had been sent back to Iowa. Could I be there for the wake, the burial? Strange that the one day I returned — in all the several thousand days since I left Iowa — was the day of Iva's final return. There is no such thing as coincidence. There is ever meaning in the patterning of our days.

I prepared myself and drove out to the settlement to pay my respects to Iva's family, then drove to the funeral home in Tama for my personal farewell. Iva's body had been dressed in traditional clothes for her journey. There were holes in her moccasins so she would not be bound here. I'd seen her only in her modest dress of t-shirt and jeans, or her shawl at powwows. Any money always went for rent and food and getting the children what they needed, and then the grandchildren, not for new clothes. I spoke to her, giving her my gratitude for all the kindnesses, the good times, and then prayed for her journey to the place in which she would not have to struggle so hard for her life.

I know I will see her again. Perhaps death and transformation are the foundation of understanding eternity. Poetry is the best tool for this.

21

Years later during a long flight from the West Coast to the east, I flew directly over Iowa City. I saw cornfields below and imagined how the winds enjoyed making a flute-like music as they blew through dried stalks in winter. I was reminded how I took to James Welch's poetry and novels to find the wryest of humor to counter dread and loss. Dread and loss are the tinder elements of humor. Oh, and those family opponents who test you most profoundly. Anything can light from it.

22

I consider my poems, stories, or music compositions as houses, or transforming stations. I must tend to the form, the architecture, even as content dictates the style, shape, and mode. The location of these houses, though they may appear in pages or in recordings, is in the liminal of the imagination. What a country that is!! The liminal of the liminal is where the most unusual forms and possibilities live. This territory is marked by the kinds of forms that live where all possibilities of light shooting through dark gather. To speak and sing a poem into place will make it stay if there is a beautiful and stunningly crafted place for it to stay.

A house is not limited to a hut, a shed, a larger single-family home, or even a vehicle. The beloved Earth can be considered a house, a house of earths, a myriad and diversity of plants, animals, rivers, waters, trees, and many kinds of living beings. The sky is the roof, made of clouds, sun, and is a place of envisioning, of calling out to helpful forces. The ocean and below-Earth are the dominion of unseen and unknown hopes and fears. In our Mvskoke cosmology these are the Middle World, the Upper and Lower World. The heart is the fire in the house that gives light. My house is the red Earth.

23

My favorite room exists now only in the imagination. That's how I visit it these days. I turn left into the yard of the small adobe house and park near the corn patch, which is by the clothesline.

I look to see if the swallow's nest is still on the porch. Then I check to see if beaks are bobbing out of the nest, as the babies look to see if someone is coming to feed them.

I knock on the kitchen door, and she lets me in, as she has done more times than I know, in many seasons of weather. It is always warm with sunlight. Dishes are drying on the side of the sink. Either she, her sister, or a niece gets me coffee. In later years she had a cane. We'd talk family, village, and Native community gossip. Sometimes we'd put on music, and everyone danced. She distrusted computers. Said they stole people. Kept their attention from what mattered. We'd walk back through the small hallway, the neat living room decorated with Pendleton blankets and Indian rugs. There were baskets, potteries, and family pictures.

I remember visiting when her mother lived there and during feast days when the house filled with tables of food and the commotion of serving, talking and laughter.

We'd go to her special room, the place where the medicine box lived, her herbs, the various items given to her by those she helped, and her altar.

She had a small shop in town where she worked. The numbers of street people who were predominately Native grew each year. She would feed them, find them clothes, and otherwise help any way that she could. She never turned anyone down who asked for help.

She always gave my children words and assistance to support whatever they were studying or doing. My daughter stayed with her on weekends from Indian school when I lived out of town. Through the years they loved to visit her.

Many came to her from all over the world for her teachings that were rooted in her spiritual knowledge. She had many invitations to travel and teach, but she did not want to put herself out that way. Her spiritual energy was a healing light and people were drawn to it, to her stories. Her Pueblo roots were powerful anchors to the land.

Her room was thick with song resonance. Through her eyes I came to see that all is spiritual and we either move about respectfully within it, or we are lost.

One day we went back to her room, and she pulled out her drum. We sang the song she was given when we had gone to the Sandia Mountains for cedar. Her hands were the color of the drum. They appeared to be made from the same earth. She later gave me that drum. When I sing that song for the cedar and what it brings, it reminds me of the spiritual path that sometimes appears dim in the smoke of historical deception.

One of my favorite memories in this life will be sitting outside near the corn patch on a bench, with my daughter and her little boys, my grandsons, waiting for her to drive up. The boys squat in the sandy dirt, running it through their hands. Our love for them plays about their shoulders. It catches the light of the love with which the corn was planted, with which the yard and house was tended, with which her life was lived.

24

Within and through each of us is a network of plants, animals, natural forces that nourish and give sustenance to the mind, heart, and spirit. It's important to acknowledge the ancestors and thank them, especially as we begin any endeavor. Let's acknowledge these beautiful lands that have made a place for people and nations from all over the world to come together and find a way. Let's acknowledge the original keepers of these lands. Native peoples of this hemisphere did not disappear. We are not in the past tense. Acknowledge the gift of our minds, spirits, and bodies (or should I say, body, as the Earth is one person), and remember to take good care always for these vehicles of movement into understanding, knowledge, and compassion. And ask for assistance as we write ourselves into the future, as we carry the past with us.

25

James Welch was a major Blackfeet writer and poet from Montana. His book of poems, *Riding the Earthboy 40* (Harper and Row, New York, 1971) is an American classic, as is his first novel, *Winter in the Blood*. My first in-person meeting with Jim was in Amsterdam in 1980 for the One World Poetry Festival. Poets converged from everywhere in the world, including Jamaica and Africa. Most inspiring was to meet Okot p'Bitek from Uganda, whose lyric poem *Song of Lawino* (East Africa Publishing House, Nairobi, 1969) is a world classic. A highlight for me was to get to shake hands and speak with a poet who had inspired me and connected me to the orality present in my poetry. He died shortly after that festival. Watching Linton Kwesi Johnson, the dub poet from Jamaica, perform in the Milkweg, I noted how even when he performed solo, without his band, his Caribbean patois rhythm patterns made everyone sway together. It was not deliberate but came naturally, with rhythm. Rhythm starts from the heart of every cell and is generated by earthiness and culture. It's coherence; it's the core.

Jim and I were interviewed together by the press, and I admit we were very irreverent and did not act the part of the Indians they had romanticized. Jim did not have hair down his back or feathers and beads. He was button-down, with cropped hair, and looked rather scholarly, even shy. I did not look exotic. I was ordinary. We escaped. It was Jim's birthday. We had dinner with Allen Ginsberg and his entourage, then walked all night from one end of Amsterdam to another, from the red-light district to the lobby of the hotel in a faraway area of town from where we had to call a taxi because no one would pick us up on the street at that nearly dawn hour. I learned from Jim's hanging-back wit, his appreciation of beauty, and the sideways symmetry of his stories.

During a cross-country flight, I wrote the first draft of a poem I would name "Grace" on the back of an envelope. One of the last times I saw Jim, we were guests at a (now) mythic writing conference in Grand Forks, North Dakota. The night had degenerated into mescal shots. I convinced the sponsor, the party ringleader, to swallow the worm, claimed it was an old Blackfeet/Creek tradition and we would be offended if he refused the worm. He swallowed dramatically. As I flew over Iowa, the whole state was white with snow. I recalled the time I spent in Iowa, how the sun hid up

here in the clouds, and how Iva and Jim made the story
a little easier.

26

White Buffalo Calf Woman appeared to the Lakota at a time when they needed inspiration for right living. John Fire Lame Deer wrote in his 1972 autobiography *Seeker of Visions: The Life of a Sioux Medicine Man* that in those times "They knew nothing. The Buffalo Woman put her sacred mind into their minds." She appeared to the Lakota in both a human form, as a beautiful woman, and as a buffalo. She brought to them the sacred pipe, corn, wasna (or pemmican), and wild turnip, and she taught the people many things, showed them the right way to live. When she disappeared, she said she would return every generation cycle.

I visited the white buffalo born in Janesville, Wisconsin, on August 20, 1994. The birth was understood by many as the promised return of White Buffalo Calf Woman. Shortly after the birth, on September 13, Arvol Looking Horse, caretaker of the White Buffalo Calf Woman pipe, was quoted in the *Beloit Daily News* as saying while he prepared for a ceremony at the

Janesville farm: "The prophesies are being fulfilled . . . We are starting to see a coming together of people going back to their natural ways."

There are always signs. When I lived in northern New Mexico, the story traveled the community that the face of Jesus had appeared in a tortilla. It was considered a miracle and parishioners came from all over New Mexico, even as far as Mexico, to witness the miracle, to be blessed by it. Many miracle cures were attributed to visits to the burned tortilla altar.

Perhaps a poem is a sign made manifest. Certainly, they can be miracles. Ask any poet.

A miracle occurred once in an Indian bar in Milwaukee. It was told to me one night as I sat in that bar with the locals, all of us tipping back our drinks with youthful bravado. It had begun snowing; a blizzard was predicted. The way it was told to me was that it was a night just like that one, in the middle of the week, no payday in sight, just the regulars. The door opened and a mysterious young Indian woman in a red dress suddenly appeared. The wind blew the door shut, a snowdrift formed, and she walked through to the counter, to order a drink. No one knew her. She didn't look like she belonged to the local Indian families, but she was Indian. Her beauty gleamed and her startling red dress spun and shone in the yellow lights of the bar.

The regulars elbowed one another, daring each other to be the first to ask her name, to find out where she came from, and who her family was. The women bunched up as they eyed their competition. She ordered another drink, then walked to the jukebox and punched in a few songs with a quarter. She stood there with a drink until her picked song began its wail. It was a popular country western tune by Kenny Rogers, not the usual worn-out rock of the regular crowd. Then, this was the miracle. She stood on a chair and climbed up on a table in front of the music. She danced and as she swayed, she took off her clothes. First her thin coat, not warm enough for a Wisconsin winter, then her shoes, her dress, then everything. She danced as Rogers sang how his beloved *Lucille* left him *with four hungry children and a crop in the field.* No one could believe the vision. This was a crowd that had seen everything — their lands stolen, starvation, massacres, children taken away and returned shorn of memory . . . everything. They were all stopped by the miracle. When the song was over, the spell was shattered. The red-dress woman was naked and shivering. An older woman who would otherwise have been home watching her grandchildren helped her get dressed. All the men ran over to the jukebox, fed it with quarters, and punched that song for replay.

I always wondered what happened to her, after her

dance on the sticky, worn table in the bar, on a night when the bar was the only place open for miles around, when no flights were coming in and out and the powerlines had all fallen. Did she make it home? How did anyone make it home? Did she make it to where she was going? Did someone lend a hand or was she ambushed?

I've kept a place in my heart for her all these years. In that place she shines and spins because she is nourished, her children are returned to her because she went through rehab. Her family stopped drinking, came together as they practiced ceremonies they had walked away from after they were deemed evil by those earliest Indian schools and churches. When I remember her, I see tall stands of pine trees around a clear, deep lake. It is early in the morning and the sun is casting flickers of light through the trees. I can hear her singing.

27

I often think in oppositions. I don't know why I am wired this way. It could be the effect of cultural impasse or collision, so my writing attempts to find a passable road in chaos. Creation and destruction, then, must find a way to come to the fire together and get to know each other.

There are many versions of the creation story. In one Mvskoke version the ground opened, and the people came out. The Wind Clan people were the first to emerge. Henry Marsey Harjo, my great-grandfather, was of the Wind Clan, my great-grandmother Katie Monahwee of the Tiger Clan. Because clan association traditionally comes through the mother, my father's mother was the Tiger Clan. She passed this clan on to him, and I am associated with this clan.

If there are creation stories, then there are destruction stories, or stories of endings that put to rest a particular episode of living. In Greek (not Creek) mythology, Charon is the ferryman of Hades, the world of the dead. He helps new souls cross over the River Styx. The souls must have been given proper ritual or they are not allowed to cross. That left a lot of souls wandering.

I wonder if Earth is the major wandering station. I often find myself in the state of questioning, which is much like wandering, in a state nowhere near Oklahoma. Poetry is my canoe. The cracks through which I fell became sheaves of lightning.

28

The first song I wrote came from grief, a wailing by a community for someone who gave up everything to pursue justice. The need for justice was a primary motivator of my first urge to write poetry. Our words had to matter. And what better way to make them sharp as arrows than with poetry.

In February 1976, an unidentified body of a young woman was found on the Pine Ridge Reservation in South Dakota. The official autopsy attributed death to exposure and alcohol. Against normal protocol the FBI agent present at the autopsy ordered her hands severed and sent to Washington for fingerprinting. This was a deliberate mutilation, what John Trudell rightly called "an act of war." Her unnamed body was buried without family, without ceremony. When Anna Mae Pictou Aquash, a young Mi'kmaq woman, an active American Indian Movement member, was discovered missing by her friends and relatives, a second autopsy was demanded. She had been killed by a bullet fired at close range to the back of her head, not alcohol consumption and exposure as had been reported. I had seen Anna Mae from a distance, at a Native rights gathering somewhere in the Southwest. She was forthright, funny, and following a vision that took her far from her home and her children.

Ten years later I was studying jazz in Denver. I wrote a poem to commemorate her life, her purpose. I wrote to hold memory, so that those coming up, my children and grandchildren, would not forget her, would not forget our struggles for justice in a country that had been nearly 100 percent indigenous and, within a few years, reduced to one-half of 1 percent indigenous.

And a few years after that I pulled out this poem, to craft music to hold it, to carry it even further into a healing. The Sisseton Wahpeton Dakota attorney and drummer Susan M. Williams and I wrote the song and performed it at the KUNM radio station in Albuquerque. That began the era of our band that became known as Joy Harjo and Poetic Justice, an all-Native band of a poet and mostly Native attorneys, all working for justice, with poetry and music. My saxophone was my singing voice.

29

When I began writing poetry, I looked to how poetry expressed itself in Mvskoke cultural traditions. When I bent close, I saw poetry everywhere, in oratorial forms, in music, and even in books. And like beadwork designs in the shape of plants with whom we have relationships, our speaking and singing structures find similar patterns and shapes. There is repetition, and even the repetitions are varied slightly just as the leaves that make a whole plant are varied and different. I discovered that poetry is never far away from music or dance.

Like the Sugpiaq anthropologist Sven Haakanson, who, when looking to assist in restoring his tribal culture, traveled to Siberian indigenous communities that still lived traditionally, I traveled in books to African poets, listened to the words of griots to understand how orality was maintained despite being translated into the format of written language.

In our root communities, where most poetry is oral rather than written down, music and dance are essential to the process of making and performing poetry. Later, when captured in written word, the music and dance are more like rhythmic shadows that enliven silence.

30

I remember the poignancy of the night desert through which I had driven as I entered a darkened, nearly empty movie theater and sat there alone with my popcorn and drink and watched a version of the life story of Charlie Parker, jazz saxophonist, one of this country's premier jazz artists. Brilliant art often finds its way through the chaos of history and human failure. Often the best artists have failed in every other area of their lives.

After watching Parker's struggle, a version of it, I wrote the line: "Some of us are born with nerve endings out to here / farther than his convoluted scales could reach."

Jazz musicians create and perform from the realms of what can't be seen but heard. They move around within constructions of a language that isn't linguistic but symbolic, even geometric. Their art is linear even as it is circular. Worlds unfold as we follow the unfolding progressions of angular storytelling. This is an American music, made from the contradictions of what is America. The band knows the shape and they exploit it together. Each musician contributes individually to make it work, even as they move together in rhythm.

Everyone has a story.

Parker's mother has a story, his father, his generation, his hometown, the breaking down, his horn, his horn case, the times, those oracular scales have a story, and there are so, so many versions.

I left that theater after the larger-than-life storytelling, the music running through me as if each of the vignettes in music were tributaries from the origin story of my heart.

The night was darker. The moon had turned over on its side. A night bird sang in the bluest distance.

31

Emerging from a story, a poem, the Earth, a time in history, or from the body of our mothers is sometimes explosive, chaotic, frightening, yet always awe-inspiring and humbling. We can use the energy to create fresh structures, or we can destroy or be destroyed. The energy can have power over us or empower us, and even what is destructive might clear the debris so that fresh life can emerge from embers or ashes. Giving birth to a poem, a story, a song, or other creation, especially a child, is a similar process, wherever and however it happens. There is a need, an intent, an urge which is given impulse by passion and belief. Sometimes you dig it out. Other times it appears from apparently the somewhere of nowhere. You are amazed that there is a line, some phrasing, a melody. You ride it out. You listen. And you become, as nothingness forms into a creation that has mobility and will move out into the world, eventually with or without you.

32

My daughter Rainy Dawn was born within a year after I began writing poetry seriously. (Though come to think of it, I always wrote poetry: seriously.) I connect her becoming with the becoming of poetry. I had great anticipation of her arrival even as my life was in questionable circumstances. I was single with a son (and sometimes a stepdaughter) and lived tenuously with her father who engaged intimately with a continuous stream of other women. He was sometimes sober, sometimes not.

To be pregnant and give birth in these circumstances made an anxiety sea. However, that she was arriving gave me tremendous happiness. In preparation for her, I painted every wall in my small, rented apartment, went to school, made art, and wrote poetry at night.

Because her father and I were poets, we had quite a discussion over her name. Because we lived in the desert and rain is precious, we named her Rainy Dawn, because there is always the promise of hope and new beginnings at dawn.

Titling is the naming of a poem. It is a doorway to meaning and marks the beginning of a ritual that a poem makes.

I do not start with titles, rather usually come back to them, as I don't always know where a poem will go, though I am aware of the impetus and have a sense of the direction we might travel. I say "we" because in the making of ritual there are mythic underpinnings and cultural manners. These are helpful forces. These shift when the language is not your original language, especially if there is an effort to translate and create concurrently.

Then we are led through the poem, by line, phrase, form, content, until we must turn to leave. If the poem is effective, if the ritual of it evokes change, then we are changed and may even carry the poem with us, through time and memory.

I have come to understand that the poem I wrote by the name of "Rainy Dawn" is also a poem to bring rain when it is needed in the desert.

33

The Salt River, or Rio Salado, flows through Tempe, Arizona. Josiah Moore, a Tohono O'odam and Pima educator, leader, and friend, told me that the river was a historical gathering place for his people. He remembered when the banks were lined with cottonwoods, when horses and wagons lined up along the river, as the people, plants and animals enjoyed the cool oasis. In the early 1980s the river was dammed and captured in Lake Roosevelt. What remained was a winding, dusty ditch that became an angry river when urgent rainstorms arrived every rainy season. Now water is flowing there again because it was good for business.

Rivers carry culture and memory, as does poetry. The poetry of this river is not an easy poetry. It too has been colonized. Then found its way again to feed cottonwoods.

34

There are sacred places on this Earth, places that generate power, that hold and even protect power. People are drawn to these places, including "power" companies that translate power into economic terms. Assisi, the home of Saint Francis, is one of these places. I was familiar with Saint Francis because as a high-school student at Indian school I often walked by the Saint Francis Cathedral in Santa Fe and read the plaque under the statue of Saint Francis. I learned that he is considered by Catholics to be the patron saint of animals, that he lived between the years of 1182 and 1226 and was the co-founder of the Franciscan Order. He was born into a wealthy family but denounced his father's wealth in 1206. Francis then began to live as a simple hermit, a lifestyle that included love and respect for all life. He composed a famous poem, the "Canticle of Brother Sun," in which he praises the Sun and Moon and Stars as living beings, as well as Wind and Air. He saw love

(God) in all living things, which was quite heretical in those days, even in these days.

The power of that love as it revealed itself in Saint Francis remains a perceptible aura of transcendence in Assisi. I was stunned by the presence of it when I visited in 1998. It is a palpable power field, especially in the small chapel built by him and his followers, and in the fields and trees of the countryside. It is still there, centuries later, transforming the world. That love blew me open to question how our word creations, tempered by fierce belief, are brokering stations that step up power. In Assisi was the first time I ever felt such evidence of love in the structure of a church. Yet the source of the light, the power, came from the countryside on which the church was built, from the sun, the moon, the connection of all life including the plants and animals. This is my understanding of the meaning of power, of Saint Francis.

When sainted, mere humans become timeless, larger than life. When a saint appears in a poem, the heaviness can sink the poem and it will never recover.

During the writing of one of my poems, I discovered Saint Coincidence, a saint who presides over incidents that appear to be coincidence. Such incidents can appear miraculous, marked by perfect timing. I did not know of a Saint Coincidence until I traveled into a creative space, made by breath, quiet, and attention. And there he stood, Saint Coincidence, a kind of lackadaisical saint who was not killed by swords or tortured for his belief. He won his sainthood by coincidence. That is another story that I do not have in this book on writing. I will need writing to get to it. In that story are perfectly petaled roses appearing in snow, a lost orphan, and an unclimbable mountain.

Or ask Sandra Cisneros about Saint Coincidence. She is a devotee.

35

One morning I began to move about our encampment to get ready for ceremonies. The Speaker, who circled the grounds to remind the people what we were doing there and why, stopped just outside our camp and proclaimed: *We do not need your university books here, your educations that take you away from what is important. Leave them outside this circle. They do not belong here.* Then he moved on, talk-singing in an oratorical style of our people, as we straightened up, pulled out our ribbon dance outfits, and got ready for the new day, the new year. Sometimes when I write poems or songs, I try to capture the sense of that style of speaking that is somewhat melodic, rhythmic, and usually carries import about what matters, always a kind of reminder of who we are and how to act. Wide approximations of that style would be southern Black orators, like preachers, and community leaders like Martin Luther King. Hawaiian chants also remind me of our oratory. The speaking ritual makes a respectful space, allows for duty, and encourages artistry in voice and delivery.

Most of us Native students attending the University of New Mexico were first-generation university students, within a generation of orality. Some of our family members were kept home to be raised in the indigenous equivalent of university. That training can be more rigorous than any university degree.

In our Native student club, one student was in line to be the next spiritual leader of his people. He discovered it was relatively easy to hide out in American culture. Yet he would return to take his place. Eventually, we all make it home, and we each make an individual path by any means. My path is made of poetry and music, characterized by rowdiness and sunflowers, and given life by everyone I have met along the way in this process of becoming human. (When I say "everyone," I don't mean just us ornery two-legged beings.)

In the end, no matter what happens, and no matter if our homes have been burned or taken over behind us as we are walked west at gunpoint, we return to the origin story, the place of the bones of our elders and ancestors. The origin story becomes the last song, encircling us with a meaning that is sometimes beyond understanding.

36

The original use of the word *songline* refers to the Australian Aboriginal concept of enforcing relationship to the land, to each other, to ancestors via the mapping of meaning with songs and narratives. Bruce Chatwin suggested in his 1987 book *The Songlines* that the whole of Australia could be read as a musical score, where a musical phrase is like a map reference.

I do not want to co-opt the term songline from the Aboriginal people. I do not have a direct explanation, just what I found in a book, nor have I asked permission. However, I know there were songs sung when this part of our existence was planted. Each of us is a song. That song was carried from the beginning of creation, an ember carried from the original ancestor of our mother line. All has been sung and is being sung into existence. I do not separate poetry from singing. Every sunrise is sung and makes a continuous dawning all over the world. It connects all of us, daughters

and sons, by thought, by heart, and on and on all of us:
humans, animals, plants, planets, universes, deity.

37

A world ended a few days ago when there was a head-on collision on an interstate in the middle of the country and a beloved daughter was killed. My words, the words of her parents, the words of her grandparents, her community, cannot bring her back. We can only grieve this teenage girl of beauty, verve, whose life spirit cast a shining path before her. Her path was unnaturally cut. And we can find no words that will make sense of this broken path, that will give insight, show us where she went, and most of all why, and why again because she is not the first.

If I make a word path of a spiral it moves through time differently than a vehicle moving in a straight line on the highway that brought death. The spiral is a continuum of motion. It is a kind of wave catcher.

This is the only possible shape, I think, as I write to find a doorway to walk through where the story will be illuminated.

We who take breath here emerge, we learn to walk, run, and engage with that which challenges us, with always a light inside that will show us the path.

When she broke on Earth, the light in her was not broken. We cannot break light, nor can we destroy it.

Let these words be eyes for us to see. Let these words be ears for us to hear.

Let these words allow us to taste the bitterness so we can know sweetness without question.

Let these words allow her family to hold her again.

Let these words remind us that she was one of us and that the circle that makes us family is a spiral. There is no end to it. We are in a continuum of embrace.

When the world as we knew it ended, we stood up again in the ruin, and found a way to keep walking through tears.

(For Alexie)

38

Every poem is a prayer, a supplication in the cacophony of humanity. There are more words now than ever, and there are so many so fast on the internet and being texted that they have lost their innate power. They are not cared for, and so many are lost and scattered. I am lonely for lullabies sung at night, I am lonely for the man singing beautifully out of tune on the street up to the window framing a beloved, I am lonely for the first words of the baby and the toothless smile of accomplishment that follows, lonely for the speaker bringing us all in to the circle together by clan and ceremonial ground, lonely for the voice of a mother who plants poetry in her children, lonely for the sound of wind in the corn plants that have been sung to as they rise up from seedlings to god figures beneath the sun.

There are some words I would like to call back. There are words that have been knives of separation, words of treaties that stole land and children, words of contracts that have taken the last cents from the poor, demeaning words, cutting words, words meant to destroy, words that took you so far away from me, my beloved.

I will use words to call my spirit back. These words are made of mists of myth, made of architectures of restorative history, made of ancient songs of coming together that lift us over and through to beauty, so that nothing or no one can ever be lost or uncared for again, now, or forever.

39

In a Miskito village near the Caribbean side of Nicaragua, the only way to translate revolutionary fervor into something useful was to feed the starving children. They suffered from malnutrition. Their native land, their country, had become a battlefield between the Contras and the Sandinistas. They were collateral.

Poetry can be written to praise despots and killers, even as it can be written to open the doors to eternity. What use is poetry, the culture bearers asked, when we do not have running water, houses, or enough food?

Then we put down our pens and paper, our writing implements, and picked up a shovel.

Late at night, when the dreams came down to dance with us, we took care of them, gave them a place to live in our poetry.

It is only nearly forty years later that I am writing about that moment, when I was a witness of history. I remember the children so tired from nursing hunger

they stood back and watched the politicos shake hands
and make promises.

Then, we left.

40

In my community, we are taught that leadership qual-ities include humility, compassion, a sense of fairness, the ability to listen, preparation and carry-through, a love for the people, and a strong spiritual center that begins with a connection to Earth. So many of our sto-ries are built around what happens to braggarts, bullies, and those who are greedy and want only for themselves.

When a despot ineptly sought to turn a country to a totalitarian nightmare, where was poetry? It wasn't sleeping. It kept the poets up at night. We wrote against despair toward beauty, toward a truth that could imprison us for making liars out of the fools depos-ited in the seats of power, kept there by puppets who kneeled in piles of promissory notes.

As I wrote, I knew that the trickster *Cufe,* or Rabbit, was somewhere nearby, kicking up dirt as he made his way from some mess or other that he started in order to show us who we are in the story of forgetfulness. As we wrote, we witnessed democracy dangled from the steps of justice by an armed mob. A viral pandemic elbowed through the barrier of hatefulness to infect us — we who thought we had a drug for everything.

And the poets kept listening, and writing.

41

I lay my body down. My mind does not slow for sleep. It has no place to rest, not in this country, this government, this time of the heavy turning Earth. An eternity can exist in a moment, an hour, or in the song bodies of humble sparrows who dream in the tree of life as it breaks through concrete and sorrow. Five trains cross downtown Tulsa. The man chased by demons screams out. He roams this area day and night. His bad dreams never sleep. They beg our ears for mercy. A ruined goddess dressed in streetlight begs a ghost for change. She wears a crown of cigarette smoke.

Tulsa is the corrupted form of the Mvskoke name for "town" or "old town": *Tallasi,* or *Tvlvhasse.* Down the street the ashes of the fires we carried in the forced march from the Southeast were rekindled beneath the Council Oak Tree. The tree is still there, our rooted story, holding in place the memory of fire.

Now a pandemic haunts these lands and the

keepers of these lands. Those viral killers approach my mind to plant fear. They act familiar, shake hands, make treaties. They sit down without being invited. We recognize them as part of the great disturbance.

I give my mind the task of holding the door open for the ancestors, the guardians, the winds. When I sing poetry there is no way in for evil.

Once in the middle of the country in the early of my life, I drove my children through the night in our small pickup, back from a winter break in Tulsa, north to Iowa City for the beginning of the spring semester. We stopped for gas just before Kansas City.

Cold winds had blown and blasted us for hours. Snow was now drift-walking the highway.

My son slid out to clean the windshield. The baby yawned then sleep-talked: "I was just dreaming someone somewhere else, and I wonder if someone somewhere else is dreaming us."

Then she went back to the origin place of poetry, the eternal road between myth and the ordinary, between history and odyssey.

We filled up with gas, kept driving through the icy darkness.

Now here we are together on the verge of shift, in our drive through what feels like the endless night of uncertainty. Nothing will be the same when this is over.

What will we know when this page is done? Who will we be? Will we survive the fires, the hatred, the heat, the rage? The sickness has taken so many.

In our ceremonial ground community, we have lost several culture-carriers. Others are on ventilators, turning toward the next sacred story. We have lost so many to acts of hatred and fear, not just now but since the beginning of this story we call "America."

The pandemic has shown us just how far away we have been from ourselves. Now we need to figure out where we are going together and how to get there, together.

42

Songs don't like to be alone. They attract others and inspire new music. I often think of music as an ocean of wild and yearning spirit. It does not behave to linear time. It is the stuff of communication between the realm of human beings, including bird-humans, other animal-humans, insect-humans, and so on. The fragmented and fragmentary poetry by urban American poets could be the natural creation of poetry shards, for a world broken apart.

43

I do not understand this path of writing. I take on this task, and as I do, I take up faith and wear it as a shield. Each time I must keep my eyes open and see what I do not want to see. Keep my ears open and hear what might be difficult to hear. Keep my heart open and know what I thought I could never do. This — every time I pick up a pen or place my hands on the keyboard to write.

To write is to make a mark in the world, to assert *I am.* There is no I without the vertical of family or poetry ancestors. There is no I without the horizontal of the community that includes trees, other plants, animals, the forces of water, air, sunlight, and all other Earthly beings. I mark the doorway with ink marks. The doorway is imagination.

In first grade we were introduced to writing. My awareness of marks making sense before I could read circles back to opening children's books to be read to, or it was the Bible, the only book in our home. I remember the Little Golden books, brightly illustrated, thin, cheaply bound, twenty-five cents per copy on a rack in the local grocery store where my mother bought groceries on credit every week as she paid off the bill for the previous week.

We didn't have extra money for books, and my mother did not take us to the library. I did not share her trepidation when it came to books and higher learning.

I ride my consciousness and ask it to take me to the first place in this life I became aware of the power of words, of how sound formed itself in words and music. This isn't the first time I've asked. I stall out here. Perhaps there was never a time that I was not aware of the power of words. Perhaps I am a body created by words, a body of words and of word-making.

I lose words when I feel lost in a wash of tasks. Like now, when the most poignant moment of the day is stepping out the back door of the apartment building to the parking lot, then down the stairs to take out the trash.

The sky is piled with cloud beings, the air humid and hot, the center of the universe thick with visitors. I have missed speaking with the clouds. They speak in poetry, in metaphor.

44

That's a story walking along the highway.

Semi passes him up, then we go by
Messy-haired kid in his party clothes
Sunday morning, hangover
Leftover from Saturday
The earliest hours of a thin moon
All the wishes and promises
In his back pocket
Spilled onto the floor
Next to a Native girl
Who said no and meant no
As she left him mid spin

In her dream, she rises
In the seat of justice
Smacks down the gavel
For order and all the missing women
Return for the honor dance

In red jingle dresses
Everyone has enough
To eat, a home.

There's a story along this trail
Of tears. We're headed east
We're going home
We left the party years ago.

45

Dreams have always appeared as doorways. They sustained me as a child and all my years growing up. They are still here to accompany me as I accumulate years, songs, poems, and stories. Each is part of a storehouse of Earthly knowledge of successes and failure.

Once a story was given to me in a dream, after a moral impasse in a creative-writing teaching job. I called out to the dark, "How do I change the story"? That night the dreaming took me to that deep inner pool of stories that are most useful when brought into the light. As artists, we are on alert for such insights because our art demands that we are challenged, never comfortable. We often find ourselves at aesthetic, artistic crossroads. Then we need our dreams to show us the way to change the story. We dream not only as individuals, but also as a collective.

46

During the dark period of Covid isolation, I went inside and to the inside of inside, and even inside of that inside. From there came new songs. From there came a series of stories and memories that I crafted into a form called "memoir," of memory. From there I continued dreaming.

One dream came to me as I was near the end of story-making for the memoir. It was one of those dreams that stands apart because it carries light. I saw myself standing at the doorway of time. I was holding a child of the seventh generation in my arms. I adjusted the blanket to see her face, to see what this one was bringing with her to share. It is in the manner that I have taken every child, grandchild, and great-grandchild into my arms to welcome them, to bless them during my time walking on the Earth. I smiled at this girl who looked at me with her eyes that shined with the memory of the place she was coming from, and with hope for the story she would make here. I thought, she looks Japanese. I told her, "You look like my daughter Rainy, your sixth great-grandmother."

I sang into the baby a song that would give her strength, and sustenance, a song that would call her ancestors to stand behind her, no matter the trials, no matter history and heartbreak.

Then I walked with her into time and delivered the baby to the Earth story that needed her.

Someone always accompanies each child born into this Earthly realm.

47

The most powerful poetry is birthed through cracks in history, through what is broken and unseen.

It is the one-hundred-year anniversary of the Tulsa Race Massacre. It occurred just a few blocks away from where I am living, where the wealthiest Black community in the country in 1921, called Black Wall Street, was burned down and many of its residents killed by white citizens who were fueled by racism and hatred.

As the search goes on for mass graves, poems are being commissioned and written as testimony and witness, so this act will not go unremembered, unspoken—so maybe the future generations will listen and take heed.

During this time, I keep returning to Natasha Trethewey's poem "Imperatives for Carrying on in the Aftermath" for illumination, to give ritual to grieving, for moving on. The poem asks us to look into our heart, and offers a folk saying learned from a Korean poet in

Seoul: "that one does not bury the mother's body/in the ground but in the chest, or—like you—//you carry her corpse on your back."

There are many corpses on the back of this country, and we will continue to carry them until we have the right tools, the right words, to bury them, so that the fertile human field of becoming can flower with justice and equality.

48

Where do we come from? Where do we go? And what of politics, war, and love? And why? What is the sense of it all? Will we ever make it home?

We all have these same questions, no matter our culture, country, generation, or age.

It is the singers, poets, and storytellers who are captured by the expression of this eternal human drama, and with language, metaphor, timing, and melody create meaningful shape. What is repetitive and ordinary becomes flowers blooming in a blizzard. A doorway appears where a door was not possible, and through it runs a white rabbit with a watch, or a white buffalo who is a promise made by mythic female power. We are terrified or delighted and with poetry, music, and story we are given a way to speak it, to understand it. We find a way through even when there appears to be no light.

It is in this time of wars, loss, pandemic, a divided nation, that we search for what singers, poets, and storytellers bring forth. We are hungry for prophets, even as we are given to despair as we turn to forgetfulness.

Each generation bears its own network of tales. Being a poet, a musician, or storyteller is not a career. It is a calling, a demand by your spirit to speak to the truth of an age, an appeal to assist justice in finding a home, for healing to take place so the succeeding generations are greeted with an abundance of food, beauty, and fresh air and water.

We must take care to feed the minds, hearts, and spirits of those coming up behind us—to offer songs, poems, and stories that will break open that which is hardened, expose that which is evil-minded or would harm, and remind us how we are constructed to bring forth beauty of thought and beingness.

My mother was the first songwriter I knew; Emily Dickinson was the first poet and my grandmother the first storyteller. From my mother I learned that songs could hold heartbreak. From Emily I learned that the immense silences I found within me were navigable by words and metaphor. From my grandmother who had no radio, no television, I learned that stories could emerge out of the deepest layers of the imagination and give themselves over to a young woman raising seven children in a sharecropper shack, who would use them to nourish her children's minds.

As I write about my grandmother, I hear a woman singing. Nearby a dog circles in the dirt, barking. There are children laughing as they run through, the sashes of the dress of one of the girls dragging on the ground from playing horse.

I see a battlefield. It is Vietnam, Afghanistan, or Horseshoe Bend. A young man heaves with nausea at the metallic smell of death and gunpowder. Blood pools around his head. Even at his young age he has heard how your life passes before you as you die. His life, however, surprises him as it turns forward in the dream field, his body gasping for breath.

The girl in the village is the color of warm brown earth, with kind eyes that shine with love for him. When they first lay down together, before he went to war, their love made roots that dove into the ground and caressed the stones. These roots find water where water is needed. When he loves her, it is with every part of his body, from his planted feet to his head good with numbers.

Those nights of early love he spoke to her when she was sleeping. His words were the vision of an architect of dreams. He told her how he would treasure her, how they would walk through this life to the next with each other, no matter the tests and disappointments that befall a human on this Earthly road. Those words blossomed into flowers, waters, and sunrises.

After the war, they married, had children, then grandchildren. They have buried parents. It has been years. They lay down together to sleep, in their grown-old bones, their weathered skins. She is a woman made of words. He is a man impatient with words. He reaches across time for her hand as he lays mortally wounded on the battlefield. They hold hands in the dark and fall asleep together. Then, he is gone.

Where do we go? And who were we fighting for, and why?

It is here that I let go, perch in front of a page and begin to sing on paper, to find myself in the story again.

49

Every place has guardians whose responsibility it is to tend that person or place. There are guardians of cities, mountains, plants, and animals, for all beings and states of mind on this planet Earth. These guardians are real and in healthy societies they are active. When the guardians, or keepers, of these lands are forcibly removed, massacred, and their lifeways stolen through the theft and warehousing of children, when female power is no longer standing equal with male power, then the lands suffer. We all suffer. The waters become polluted, fires are out of control, storms become massive and aggressive, and the Earth trembles. There is confusion and destruction among all those who inhabit the land, these times.

But we can change the story—and that is done by the artists, the thinkers, and the dreamers, those who can envision from within this immense field. Indigenous artists must be part of the leadership in the revision of the American story. We can change the story of a violent hierarchy that follows in the wake of the papal bulls proclaiming indigenous peoples as non-humans for land and resource theft and slavery, to Manifest Destiny, which opened the West and the world for the taking, and set in place a caste system that places value according to skin color, culture, sexual identity, and economic standing. We can turn to honoring female power, without whom there is no life. Rivers, mountains, lands, other animals, and elemental inhabitants will be respected co-inhabitants.

Time, experience, and the ancestors have taught me that it is while practicing our arts and in ceremony that we come closest to who we really are, as individuals, as part of a family, a generation, a country, a planet, a timeless point of experience. It is then we come into close contact with our ancestors, the origin. We must feed that place, honor it.

I bow down to the story keepers, to the keepers of poetry. I am reminded of the water spider, who when the Earth was covered with water, carried an ember on her back so we could make fire to keep the story going. Everything is a prayer in the becoming as she approaches us, swimming through time.

50

You are a story fed by the generations.

You carry songs, grief, triumph, thankfulness, and joy. Feel their power as they ascend within you. As you walk, run swiftly, even fly, to infinite possibilities.

Let go of that which burdens you. Let go of any acts of unkindness or brutality.

Let go of that which has burdened your family, your community, your nation. Let go of that which has disturbed your soul. Let go one breath into another. Pray thankfulness for this Earth we are — Pray thankfulness for this becoming we are —

For this sunlight touching skin we are — For this cooling by the waters we are —

Listen now as Earth sheds her skin. Listen as the generations move one against the other to make power. We are bringing in a new story. We will be accompanied by ancient and new songs and will celebrate together.

I was a reluctant writer. I tend to see the forest, all the layers of possibility, all time, which makes it very difficult to focus, because I can get lost and not know where to start, and how will I know everything? The most powerful moment is just . . . starting.

Start anywhere to catch the light.